Contents

T0346067

Welcome to The Rise and Shine Library

1 Read and match. Then write.

> reading corner   gallery   courtyard   multimedia room   ~~Biscuit~~

 1 ☐ d
 2 ☐
 3 ☐
 4 ☐
 5 ☐

a I'm Rafa. I like the r_____ c_____.

b I'm Alicia. I like the c_____.

c I'm Daniel. I like the g_____.

d I'm Thomas. B iscuit _____ is my dog.

e I'm Lena. I like the m_____ r_____.

2 Think and write.

> has got   hasn't got

1 The library __has got__ a multimedia room.

2 The library _____ a bedroom.

3 It _____ a gallery.

4 It _____ an information desk.

5 It _____ a garage.

> **Tell me!**
> Where can you watch films in the library?

3 Write. Then ask and answer.

Has the library got _____?

Yes, it _____.

Has it got _____?

No, it _____.

Extra time? Have you got a library in your town or school? What has it got?

Match. Then listen, circle and write.

a beanbag
(22) / 32
twenty-two

b computer
13 / 30
_____

c television
4 / 44
_____

d poster
15 / 50
_____

Let's build!
What has your classroom got?

5 Read and draw.

It's four o'clock.

It's nine o'clock.

It's half past three.

4
It's half past eleven.

I can shine!

6 Imagine your perfect library. Think and complete.

My perfect library

It's got...	It hasn't got...

Extra time? Tell your family about your perfect library.

All about school!

Let's review! PB p7 →

Think and write.

| 25 _twenty_ -five | 38 _____ -eight |
| 67 _____ -seven | 89 _____ -nine |

Lesson 1 → Vocabulary

1 **Read and number.**

| 1 Music | 2 Art | 3 English | 4 Maths | 5 PE |
| 6 History | 7 Geography | 8 ICT | 9 Drama | 10 Science |

2 **Look and write.**

1 Science

2  _____

3  _____

4  _____

5  _____

6  _____

7  _____

8  _____

Tell me!
What school subjects use numbers?

④

Extra time? Number the school subjects from 1–10: 1 = ☺ 10 = ☹

1   Listen and circle.

Monday	History	(Maths)
Tuesday	Art	Music
Wednesday	English	Geography
Thursday	PE	Drama
Friday	ICT	Science

2 Look at Activity 1. Write.

1 What have you got on Monday?

I've got _____Maths._____

2 What have you got on Tuesday?

I've got _____.

3 What _____ you _____ on Wednesday?

I _____.

4 _____ on Thursday?

I _____.

I can shine!

3 💬 Choose a school day. Write the school subjects you've got. Then ask and answer.

Day: _____
_____
_____

What _____ on _____?

I_____ and _____.

1 Number for you. Then write.

| brush | bed | ~~wake~~ | breakfast | shower | school |

I go to _____ .   I have a _____ .   I go to _____ .

I ___wake___ up.   I _____ my teeth.   I have _____ .

2 PB p12–13 ➡ Read and answer. *True (T)* or *false (F)*?

I don't like Geography.

I've only got 19 teeth, look!

I go to bed at eight o'clock and I wake up at nine o'clock in the morning.

Yes, I think I like Maths now.

①  F

②

③

④

I can shine!

Let's imagine!
What do you think?
The story is: OK ☆   good ☆☆
great ☆☆☆

3 Write for you.

I wake up at _____ on Friday.

I've got _____ and _____ on Friday.

I like _____ .

Extra time? What things in your classroom have symmetry? Draw or write.

1 **Look and write.**

1 What time do you wake up? I <u>wake up</u> at <u>seven o'clock.</u>

2 What time _____ you have breakfast?

I _____ at half past _____.

3 _____ brush your teeth?

_____ at _____.

4 _____ go to bed?

_____

2 **Write. Then number.**

I _____ to school.

How do you _____ to school?

I go to school by _____. And you?

I can shine!

Let's build!
What time do you wake up on Saturday?

3 💬 **Draw and circle. Then ask and answer.**

What time do you wake up?

I wake up at....

How do you go to school?

Pronunciation Circle the odd word out: boy toy walk

1 **Read and match.**

Time	Monday	Tuesday	Wednsday	Thursday
9.00	Maths	ICT	Art	Music
10.00	History	Drama	English	Maths
11.00	Science	PE	ICT	Geography
12.00	English	Maths	Science	English

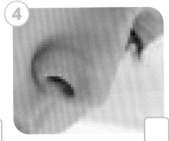

a   This is my classroom. There are twenty students in my class.

b   This is the playground. We play after lunch.

c   I do my homework at four o'clock.

d   This is my school timetable. On Monday, I've got Maths at nine o'clock.

2 **Listen and tick (✓). Then write.**

My favourite day is ¹_____Tuesday._____

I've got ²_____ on Tuesday.

I play in the ³_____ at lunchtime.

I do my homework at ⁴_____.

All children have the same school day. True or false?

Extra time? What is your favourite day at school? Why?

1 **Read and match.**

My school day, by Alex

On school days, I wake up at seven o'clock. c

I have breakfast at half past seven.

I go to school by bike.

I like Mondays. I've got Geography, PE and Drama.

I go to bed at half past eight.

a
b
c
d
e

2 Give it a go **Plan your diary entry.**

1 What time do you wake up? _____

2 What time do you have breakfast? _____

3 What time do you go to school? _____

4 What school day do you like? _____

5 What subjects have you got? _____

6 What time do you go to bed? _____

I can shine!

3 **Write your diary entry.**

My school day, by _____

On school days, I _____ at _____.

I _____.

I _____.

I like _____.

I've got _____.

I _____ at _____.

Check your work! Remember to use capital letters! Monday Friday Art Music

1 Find and circle. Then write.

A	W	Y	Q	A	M	K	L	I	M
G	A	O	I	C	T	P	H	Y	U
U	K	R	T	X	T	Z	B	V	S
E	E	B	D	F	P	G	R	O	I
N	U	W	Q	M	E	N	M	L	C
G	P	D	T	L	G	S	D	R	Y
L	L	J	H	W	S	P	S	Z	V
I	Y	G	O	T	O	B	E	D	A
S	Y	F	S	D	H	U	I	P	R
H	X	H	I	S	T	O	R	Y	T

1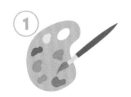

Art

2

_____

3

_____

4

_____

5

_____

6

Hello

_____

7

_____

8

_____

2 Write. Then listen and check.

1

What __have__ you __got__ at school on Monday?

I've got _____ and _____.

2

What time do you _____?

I have a shower at _____.

3

What time _____?

I have breakfast _____.

3 Write and answer for you. Then talk with a friend.

How do you go to school?   I _____.

10

Extra time? What are these school subjects?   a a D m r   e G o g a r y p h   s h t a M

1 **Think and write.**

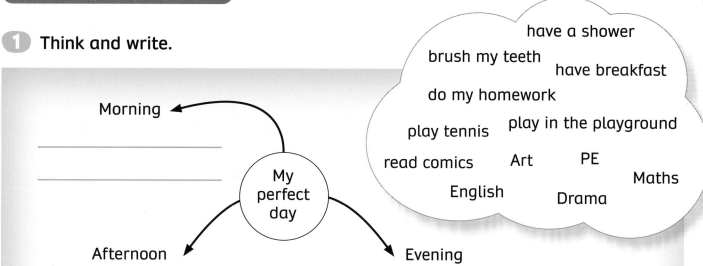

Morning
_____
_____

My perfect day

have a shower
brush my teeth
have breakfast
do my homework
play tennis   play in the playground
read comics   Art   PE
English   Drama   Maths

Afternoon
_____
_____

Evening
_____
_____

2 **Make your lapbook. Find pictures or draw. Then write.**

My Perfect Day

1 What time do you wake up? _____

2 How do you go to school? _____

3 What subjects have you got? _____

4 What do you do in the evening? _____

5 What time do you go to bed? _____

My Perfect Day

I wake up at seven o'clock.

I go to school by car.

I love Art!

I've got Art and Maths.

I go to bed at nine o'clock.

Explore our town!

Let's review! PB p10–11

Think and write.

What subjects have you got at school today?

_____ _____

_____ _____

Lesson 1 ➡ Vocabulary

1 **Read and number.**

| 1 town square | 2 hospital | 3 cinema | 4 sports centre | 5 police station |
| 6 café | 7 pharmacy | 8 bus stop | 9 supermarket | 10 shop |

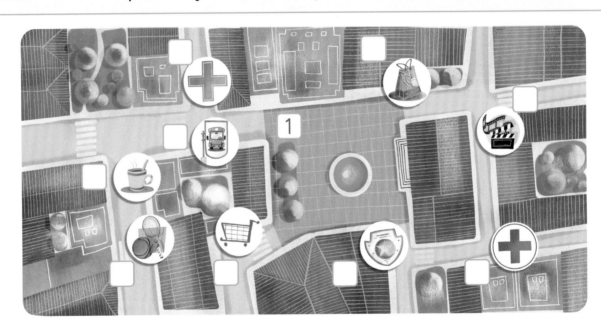

2 **Look and write.**

1

pharmacy

2

3

4

5

6

7

8

Tell me!

Where can I go when I'm hungry?

12

Extra time? What places do you go to in your town?

1 🎧 (2.06) **Listen and tick (✓) or cross (✗). Then match.**

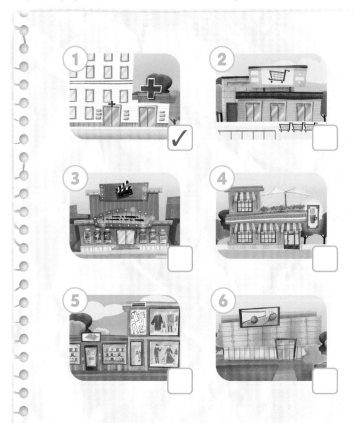

In my town...

1 there's   a   a supermarket.

2 there's   b   a cinema.

3 there isn't   c   a hospital.

4 there aren't   d   any cafés.

5 there are   e   a sports centre.

6 there isn't   f   some shops.

2 **Look and write.**

> There are some   There aren't any
> ~~There's a~~   There isn't a

1 _____There's a_____ pharmacy.

2 _____ police station.

3 _____ cafés.

4 _____ bus stops.

I can shine! ✳

3 **Write about your town.**

There's _____. There isn't _____.

There are _____. There aren't _____.

Extra time? Which new word is difficult for you?

1 **Look and write.**

| doctor   waiter   librarian   bus driver   shop assistant   police officer |

1 ___doctor___

2 _____

3 _____

4 _____

5 _____

6 _____

2 PB p22–23 **Read and match.**

1 — C

2 — ☐

3 — ☐

4 — ☐

a *What a great day!*

b *Look! There's the doctor! She's at the bus stop!*

c *There's a bookshop! Let's ask the shop assistant.*

d *Excuse me, officer! This isn't our book.*

I can shine!

Let's imagine!
What do you think?
The story is: OK ☆   good ☆☆
great ☆☆☆

3 **Write for you. Who helps you...**

at the library?
_____

at the hospital?
_____

at the shops?
_____

at the police station?
_____

Extra time? Is the doctor happy at the end of the story? Why or why not?

1 **Look and circle.**

1   Is there a police officer?
Yes, there is. / No, there isn't.

2   Is there a bus driver?
Yes, there is. / No, there isn't.

3   Are there any librarians?
Yes, there are. / No, there aren't.

4   Are there any waiters?
Yes, there are. / No, there aren't.

2 **Order and write. Then say.**

> **Let's build!**
> *Is there a bus driver?*
> *Are there any shop assistants?*

> *live? / you / Where / do*
> <u>Where</u> _____?

> *Park / live / I / on / Street.*
> _____

I can shine!

3   💬   **Think and write. Then ask and answer.**

> Is there a _____ in your town?

> Are there any _____?

> Where do you _____?

Pronunciation Circle the odd word out: there   park   where

(15)

1 Read and match.

a

a   I love my community. It's great!

b   There's a big fountain in my town square.

c   There are some benches.

d   People in my town are very friendly.

2 2.16 Listen and tick (✓). Then write.

a

b

cafés ~~town square~~ community friendly cinema fountain shops

This is my ¹ town square. There isn't a ² _____.

But there are some ³ _____ and ⁴ _____.

There's a ⁵ _____. People in my town are very

⁶ _____. I love my town and my ⁷ _____.

What do you like about your community?

Extra time? Say three things you can see in your town square.

1 What is in the sports centre? Read and tick (✓).

My favourite place, by Maria

My favourite place is the sports centre. I play tennis!

There's a café.

It's got some nice biscuits.

There aren't any shops.

I go there by bus. The bus driver helps me.

I love the sports centre!

2 Give it a go **Plan your leaflet.**

1 What's your favourite place in town? _____

2 There's a _____ .

3 There aren't any _____ .

4 Who helps you? _____

I can shine!

3 Write your leaflet.

My favourite place, by _____

There's _____ .

There aren't _____ .

There _____ .

_____ helps me.

_____

Check your work! [.] or [?]: Is there a hospital ☐   There's a hospital ☐

(17)

1 **Find and circle. Then write.**

(librarian)caféspoliceofficerswaiterspharmacyshopscinematownsquare

In my town

There's a...

librarian

_____

_____

_____

There are some...

_____

_____

_____

_____

2 **Write. Then listen and check.**

Is there a librarian?

No, there _____.

_____ there any waiters?

No, there _____.

_____ any doctors?

Yes, _____.

You're at the _____.

3 **Write and answer for you. Then talk with a friend.**

Where _____ you live?

I _____.

Extra time? You can have breakfast or lunch in this place. It's a....

1 **Think and write.**

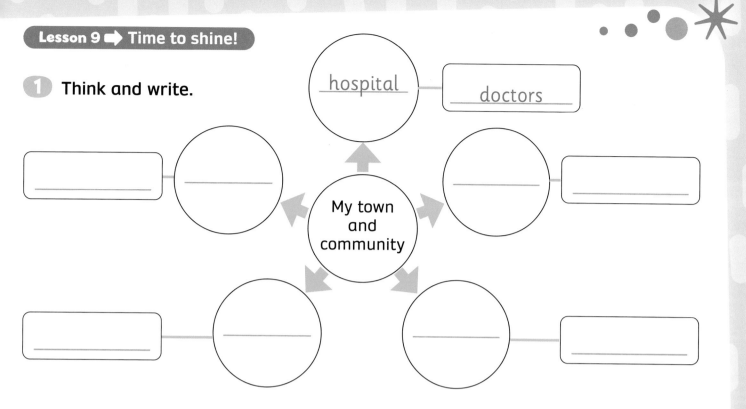

hospital — doctors

My town and community

2 **Make your lapbook. Find pictures or draw. Then write.**

My favourite people and places

1 What places are there in your town? _____

2 What are your favourite places? _____

3 Who helps you? _____

My favourite people and places

There's a library in my town.

There's a librarian. He's friendly. He helps me.

There's a hospital in my town.

There's a doctor. She helps me.

1 Look, read and write.

On Saturday, I ^{1} _wake up_ at half past eight.

I ^{2}_____ at nine o'clock.

I've got ^{3}_____ Club at half past ten.

After lunch, I go to the ^{4}_____ with my friends.

There are some ^{5}_____ and the

^{6}_____ are very friendly.

I ^{7}_____ at ten o'clock.

2 Number. Listen and check. Then ask and answer.

I go to school by bus.

Hi, Anna. Where do you live? 1

How do you go to school?

I walk to school. How about you?

I live on Green Street. And you?

I live next to the cinema.

3 Order and write. Then answer for you.

1 breakfast / What / you / time / do / have

<u>What time do you have breakfast?</u>

<u>I have breakfast at</u> _____ .

2 Friday / What / you / on / got / have

_____ ?

_____ .

3 hospital / there / Is / a / town / your / in

_____ ?

_____ .

4 any / librarians / Are / there / in / town / your

_____ ?

_____ .

Mini-project

4 Think and write.

On Sunday, I _____ .

I have _____ at

_____ .

After lunch, I go to _____ .

There's a _____ .

There aren't any _____ .

_____

Time to shine!

5 Read and tick (✓). Tell your friend.

1 I can write a diary entry about my day. ☐

2 I can write a leaflet about my town. ☐

3 I can talk about my daily routine. ☐

4 I can talk about the people and places there are in my town. ☐

My favourite song is in

Unit 1 ☐   Unit 2 ☐

My favourite story is in

Unit 1 ☐   Unit 2 ☐

6 Vote. Sing or act out.

Let's tell stories!

Let's review! PB p20–21 ⟶

Think and write.

Where can you go to...

see a doctor? _____

have lunch? _____

watch a film? _____

Lesson 1 ➡ Vocabulary

1 Read and number.

1 prince	2 superhero	3 spy	4 monster	5 giant
6 pirate	7 princess	8 astronaut	9 dragon	10 storyteller

2 Look and write.

spy

Tell me!

He's got black hair. He's tall. He can fly. Who is he?

Extra time? What characters are in your story book?

1  **Listen and tick (✓).**

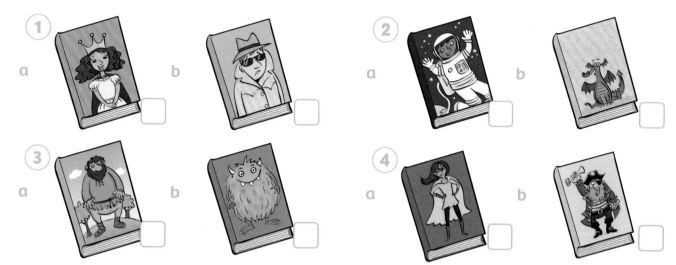

2 **Look at Activity 1. Write.**

1
The book is about a ___princess.___

_____Is_____ she happy?

Yes, she _____.

2
The book is about a _____.

_____ it big?

No, it _____.

3
The book is about a _____.

_____ tall?

Yes, _____.

4
The book is about a _____.

_____ bad?

No, _____.

I can shine!

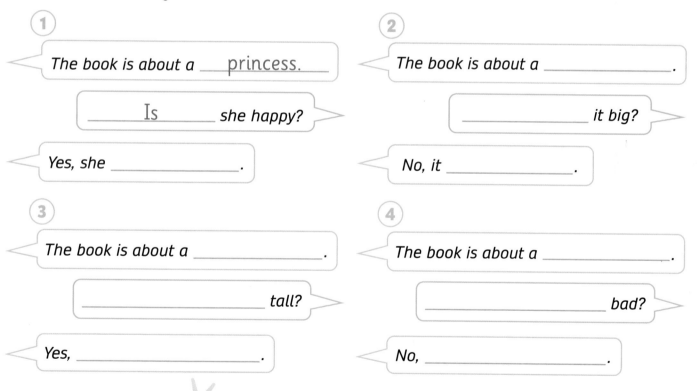

3 **Write about your favourite book.**

My favourite book is _____.

It's about _____.

Extra time? Write and spell. pir __ te   sp __   g __ ant   dr __ gon

1 Look and circle. Then write.

cute   (strong)   scary   brave   kind   clever   scary   clever

1 The astronaut is ___strong.___   3 The superhero is _____.

2 The giant is _____.   4 The spies are _____.

2 PB p34–35 Think about the story. Then read and tick (✓).

It's about a brother and a sister.
They're scary. ☐

It's about an astronaut. He's cute and clever. ☐

It's about a boy and his friends.
They share their favourite books. ☐

It's about a superhero
and a dragon. ☐

Let's imagine!
What do you think?
The story is: OK ☆   good ☆☆
great ☆☆☆

I can shine!

3 Write for you.

My favourite book character is _____.

He's / She's _____.

Extra time? Circle the books you like. I like story / adventure / sticker books.

1 **Look and write.**

1 <u>Are</u> they strong? Yes, they <u>are.</u>   3 _____ cute? _____.
2 _____ they kind? No, they _____.   4 _____ scary? _____.

> **Let's build!**
> *Ask and answer about superheroes.*

2 **Read and circle.**

I like this book about spies.

I don't like this book about pirates.

① Oh, I do! / So do I!

② Oh, I do! / So do I!

I can shine!

3 **Write for you. Then talk with a friend.**

monsters   princesses
superheroes   giants
dragons   pirates

I like books about _____.
I don't like books about _____.

So do I! / Oh, I do!

Pronunciation Circle the odd word out: brave   boy   very   book

1 Read and answer. *True (T)* or *false (F)*?

1 Opera tells stories with puppets. [F]

2 Kathak dancers tell stories with dance. The clothes are beautiful. ☐

3 Hula tells stories with dance and chants. It's from India. ☐

4 Chinese shadow puppets tell stories about dragons. ☐

2 Listen and match. Then write for you.

1 Chinese shadow puppets are   a interesting.

2 Opera is   b fun.

3 Indian Kathak dance is   c beautiful.

4 Hula dancing is   d exciting.

I like <u>Chinese shadow puppets.</u> They're <u>interesting.</u>

I like _____ .

How do you share stories in class? Do you read books together / watch films / make puppets / sing?

Extra time? At home we tell stories with….

1 **Read and tick (✓).**

My film review, by Theo
I like this film. It's great! It's about
a superhero and a giant. They're
brave and strong. There's a spy in
the story, too. He's clever and kind. I think
the story is very interesting and exciting.

2 Give it a go **Plan your film review.**

1 It's about _____ and _____ .

2 They're _____ .

3 There's a _____ .

4 He's / She's _____ .

5 The film is fun / interesting / exciting.

I can shine!

3 **Write your film review.**

My film review, by _____

It's _____ .

They _____ .

_____

_____

_____

Check your work! Write *a* or *an*: ___ spy ___ astronaut ___ prince ___ monster

1 Write the words.

①

②

③

④

⑤

⑥

⑦

⑧

⑨

	¹m	o	n	s	t	e	r		

A _____ can tell you a story.

2 (3.19) Order and write. Then listen and check.

about / book / The / is / monsters.

The book is _____.

they / scary? / Are

_____

they / aren't. / No,

_____

cute? / they / Are

_____

they / Yes, / are.

_____

3 Write and answer for you. Then talk with a friend.

I like books about _____.

So do I! I don't like books about _____.

Oh, I do!

28 **Extra time?** Is he [s o n g r t] _____ and [d i n k] _____? Yes, he is. He's a _____.

1 💬 **Think and match. Then talk with a friend.**

prince

princess

dragon

astronaut

pirate

giant

superhero

monster

cute

strong

scary

brave

kind

clever

tall

small

In my book, the _____

is _____ .

2 **Make your lapbook. Find pictures or draw. Then write.**

My story

1 What's your story about? _____ and _____

2 Describe the characters. _____

3 How can you tell your story? _____

4 Party at the library!
Let's review! PB p32-33

Think and write.

My four favourite book characters are

_____ _____

_____ _____

Lesson 1 ➡ Vocabulary

1 Read and number.

1 playing chess	2 taking photos	3 coding	4 painting
5 having a party	6 swapping cards	7 juggling	8 acting
9 playing computer games		10 learning an instrument	

2 Look, read and write.

1 I've got a camera. I like ___taking___ photos.

2 I like _____ pictures of my friends.

3 It's my birthday. I'm _____ with my family.

4 Drama is my favourite subject. I like _____.

5 I've got my violin lesson on Tuesday. I'm _____

   _____.

6 I've got three balls. I like _____.

Tell me!
*I've got a computer.
What are my hobbies?*

Extra time? What hobbies can you do with a friend?

1 Listen and tick (✓) or cross (✗).

	painting	playing chess	swapping cards	juggling
 James				
Sonia				

2 Look at Activity 1. Write.

1 James likes _painting._____

  He likes _____

  and _____.

2 He doesn't like _____.

3 Sonia _likes_____

  and _____.

4 She doesn't _____

  and she doesn't _____.

I can shine!

3 Write about your friends.

  _Alex likes acting. He doesn't like juggling._____

  ☺ _____ likes _____.

  ☹ _____ doesn't like _____.

  ☺ _____

  ☹ _____

Extra time? Order and write. Draw. coding. / Maria / like / doesn't ☺

1 Look and write.

| being | using | doing |
| helping | doing | learning |

| sport | ~~people~~ | outside |
| something new |
| crafts | computers |

1 _helping people_

2 _____

3 _____

4 _____

5 _____

6 _____

2 PB p44–45 **Read and match.**

 1 ☐

 2 ☐

 3 ☐

 4 a

a Can I help you learn something new now?

b Wait, where are Lena and Rafa?

c Don't worry, Rafa. I like helping people.

d Does Lena like doing crafts?

I can shine!

Let's imagine!
What do you think?
The story is: OK ☆   good ☆☆
great ☆☆☆

3 **Write for you.**
Choose your three favourite activities for a party.

I like _____ , _____ and _____ .

Extra time? Thomas thinks the decorations are....

1 Order and write. Then answer.

1 like / Does / acting? / he

Does he like acting?

Yes, _he does._

2 she / photos / taking / Does / like

_____?

No, _____.

3 he / games / like / Does / computer / playing

_____

_____?

_____.

4 being / she / like / Does / outside

_____?

_____.

2 Read and number.

Let's build!
Rafa / like / doing sport?

No, I'm not. I want to learn. Are you good at painting?

Yes, I am. Don't worry. You can learn!

OK. Let's go to Art Club!

Are you good at painting?

1

I can shine!

3 Think and write for you. Then talk with a friend. Find two things you both want to learn.

Are you good at _____?

Yes, _____.

OK. Let's go to _____!

No, _____.

Pronunciation Circle the odd word out: singing   thing   learn   coding

1 **Read and circle.**

1 Origami is Japanese. It means to (**fold**) / **cut** paper.

2 I paint pictures and I **cut** / **knit** them out.

3 Finger knitting is fun! I use my fingers to **stick** / **knit** scarves for my toys.

4 I **fold** / **stick** my favourite photos in my scrapbook.

2 [4.16] **Listen and match. Then write.**

origami   scrapbooks   knitting

1

I'm good at taking photos.

a

I'm good at finger _____.

2

I like making scarves for my teddy bears.

b

My favourite craft is _____.

3

I like making paper animals.

c

I like sticking photos in my _____.

What's a typical craft in your country?

3 **Choose a craft you like. Write.**

I like doing origami. I fold paper. I make flowers.

_____

Extra time? Which hobbies use paper?
finger knitting   origami   making scrapbooks   coding

1 Read and tick (✓). Then circle the instruction words.

_____ , by Monty

a

1   (Fold) a piece of card.

Make an origami animal

2   Draw a picture of flowers on a piece of paper.

3   Cut out the flowers.

b

4   Stick your flowers onto the card.

5   Write a message inside.

☐

Make a birthday card

2 Give it a go Choose a different craft. Plan your instructions.

1 I want to _____ .

2 I need _____ .

3 Instruction words I can use: _____ _____

_____ _____ _____

4 Step 1: _____ .

I can shine!

3 Write your instructions. Then draw.

Make _____ , by _____

_____

_____

_____

_____

Check your work! Check your spelling. write   knit   stick   paint

1 **Look and write.**

g i n g g l u j   t a c g i n   g i c o d n   a n i p t g i n   g l a p y i n   s h e c s

1 _juggling_   2 _____   3 _____   4 _____   5 _____

s a p p w i g n   d a r c s   g i n b e   t o u e d s i   s i n g u   p e r s m o c u t

6 _____   7 _____   8 _____

2 Listen and draw. Then write.

1

a He ___likes___ doing sport.

b He _____ learning an instrument.

c _____ he like playing computer games? _____

2

a She _____ .

b She _____ .

c _____ having a party?

_____

3 💬 **Order and write. Answer for you. Then talk with a friend.**

good / taking / Are / at / photos / you

_____ ?

_____

Extra time? It's a craft. You fold paper and you can make animals.

1 **Think and write. Then talk with a friend.**

Hobbies and crafts

Inside

_____

_____

Both

_____

_____

Outside

_____

_____

2 **Make your lapbook. Find pictures or draw. Then write.**

My favourite hobbies

1 Hobbies I like: _____

2 I'm good at _____ .

3 outside or inside? _____

4 I do them with _____ .

1 Read and write.

acting ~~kind~~ chess using clever cards

My best friend is Martin.

He's [1]____kind____ and [2]_____ .

He's good at [3]_____ computers.

I like swapping [4]_____with Martin.

He likes playing [5]_____ .

He doesn't like [6]_____ .

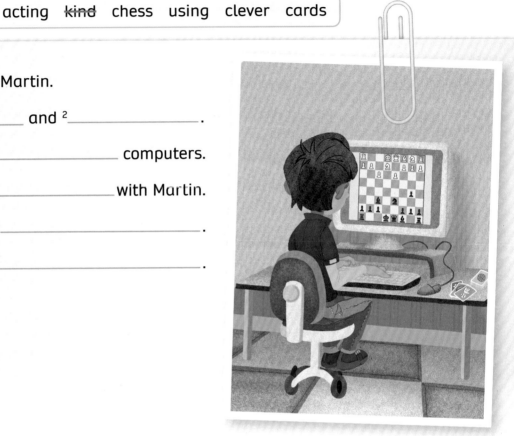

2 (4.22) Match. Listen and check. Then ask and answer.

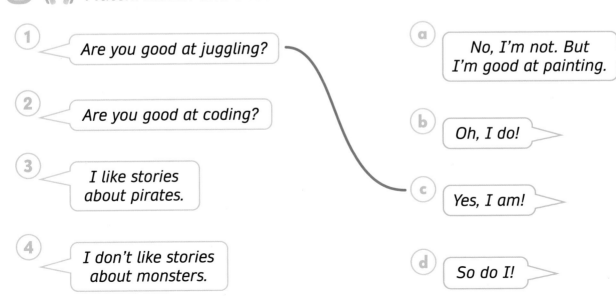

1 Are you good at juggling?

2 Are you good at coding?

3 I like stories about pirates.

4 I don't like stories about monsters.

a No, I'm not. But I'm good at painting.

b Oh, I do!

c Yes, I am!

d So do I!

3 Read and circle.

Lily   Tom

1 **Are** / **Is** they pirates? Yes, they **are** / **aren't**.

2 **Is** / **Are** they cute? No, they **aren't** / **isn't**.

3 **Do** / **Does** Tom like helping people?
Yes, he **does** / **doesn't**.

4 Does Lily **like** / **likes** being outside?
No, she **doesn't** / **do**.

5 **Is** / **Are** Tom scary? Yes, he **is** / **isn't**.

Mini-project

4 Think and write.

My best friend is _____ .

He / She's _____ .

He / She likes _____ .

He / She doesn't like _____ .

He / She's good at _____ .

I like _____

with _____ .

Time to shine!

5 Read and tick (✓). Tell your friend.

1 I can write a review about my favourite book. ☐

2 I can write instructions about how to make something. ☐

3 I can talk about books. ☐

4 I can ask and answer about what activities my friends like. ☐

My favourite song is in
Unit 3 ☐   Unit 4 ☐

My favourite story is in
Unit 3 ☐   Unit 4 ☐

6 🤖 Vote. Sing or act out.

Let's save our animals!
Let's review! PB p42–43

Think and write.

Which hobbies can you do outside?

_____   _____

_____   _____

Lesson 1 ➡ Vocabulary

1 **Read and number.**

1 monkeys	2 parrots	3 tigers	4 lions	5 leopards
6 penguins	7 pandas	8 rhinos	9 zebras	10 snakes

2 **Look, read and write.**

They're long.

They're ___snakes.___

They're fast.

They're _____.

They're black and orange.

They're _____.

Tell me!
They're black and white. They're cute.

They're big and scary.

They're _____.

They're funny.

They're _____.

They're strong.

They're _____.

Extra time? Which animals have got four legs?

1 5.06 **Listen and tick (✓). Then write.**

①

a   b

②

a   b

They ____can____ swim.

They ____can't____ walk.

They're _____ .

They _____ walk.

They _____ fly.

They're _____ .

2 **Look and write.**

1 ____Can____ they walk?

Yes, they ____can.____

2 _____ they fly?

No, _____ .

3 _____ they run?

_____

4 _____ sing?

_____

I can shine! ✳

3 **Write about your favourite animals.**

My favourite animals are _____ .

They can _____ .

They can't _____ .

Extra time? What animals start with *p* and *l*?

41

1 **Look and circle. Then write.**

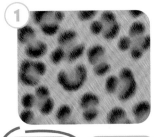  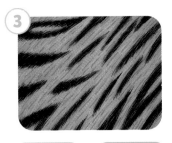 

1️⃣ (spots) stripes   2️⃣ fur feathers   3️⃣ spots stripes   4️⃣ tail wings

____spots____   _____   _____   _____

2 PB p56–57 ➡ **Read and tick (✓) for long-eared jerboas.**

a *They've got fur and spots.*
They can run fast. ☐

b *They've got long tails and big ears.*
They can jump very high. ☐

c *They've got wings and feathers.*
They can fly. ☐

Let's imagine!
What do you think?
The story is: OK ☆   good ☆☆
great ☆☆☆

I can **shine!**

3 **Choose an animal from the story. Write.**

They're _____ .
They've got _____ .
They can _____ .
They can't _____ .

Extra time? What animals in the story are cute / big / scary / strong?

1 Look, read and circle. Then write.

1 They**'ve got** / (**haven't got**)
spots. Have they got stripes?
Yes, <u>they have.</u>

2 They**'ve got** / **haven't got** legs.
_____ they _____ a tail?
No, _____.

3 They _____ wings.
Have _____ feathers?
_____

4 _____ fur.
_____ stripes?
_____

2 Read and match.

Let's build!
Say what the animals have or haven't got.

1 *Shall we learn about pandas?*

2 *Shall we watch a film?*

3 *Shall we look on the internet?*

a *Yes, that sounds great!*

b *I'm not sure. I don't like films.*

c *Sure! I like pandas.*

I can shine!

3 💬 Think and write. Then ask and answer.

Shall we learn about _____ ?   *Yes,* _____ .

Have they got _____ ?   *Yes,* _____ .

Have they got _____ ?   *No,* _____ .

Pronunciation Circle the odd word out: snake   shall   spots   stripes

43

1 **Read and circle.**

1 It's very hot in the **ocean** / (grassland.)

2 There's a lot of fruit in the **desert** / **jungle.**

3 There isn't a lot of water in the **desert** / ~~ocean.~~

4 It's cold in the **jungle** / **ocean.**

2 🎧 5.16 **Listen and match. Then write.**

a desert   **b** jungle   **c** ocean   **d** grassland

1 Penguins live in the _____ocean._____

2 Some snakes live in the _____.

3 Parrots and _____ live in the _____.

4 Rhinos and _____ live in _____.

3 **Choose an animal. Write.**

Leopards live in the jungle. _____

_____

Can you find out where pandas live?

44

1 Read and tick (✓). Then write.

My fact file puzzle, by Tessa

They live in grassland.

They've got a tail and they've got four legs.

They haven't got fur and they haven't got feathers.

They can walk, run and swim!

They can't fly and they can't jump.

They're _____.

2 Give it a go **Plan your fact file puzzle.**

1 Where do they live? _____

2 What have they got? _____, _____

3 What can they do? _____, _____

4 What are they? _____

I can shine!

3 Write your fact file puzzle.

My fact file puzzle, by _____

_____

_____

_____

_____

_____

Check your work! Remember! They've got   They haven't got   They can't

45

1 Write the words.

Down

Across

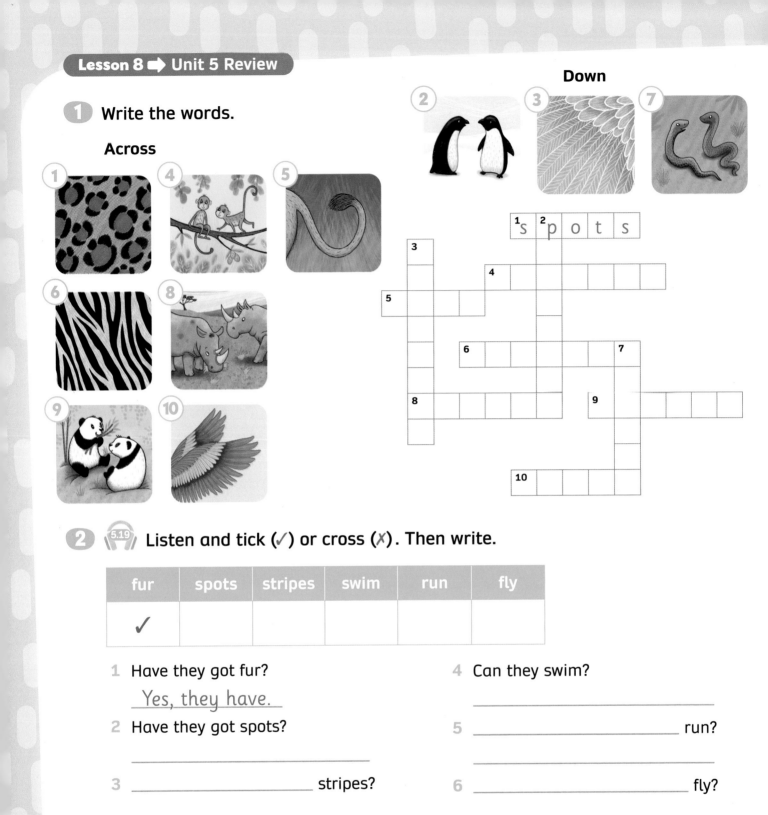

2 Listen and tick (✓) or cross (✗). Then write.

fur	spots	stripes	swim	run	fly
✓					

1 Have they got fur?
   Yes, they have.
2 Have they got spots?
   _____
3 _____ stripes?
   _____

4 Can they swim?
   _____
5 _____ run?
   _____
6 _____ fly?
   _____
   They're _____.

3 Order and write. Answer for you. Then talk with a friend.

Shall we watch a film about pandas?

not / sure. / I'm
_____

great / That's / idea! / a
_____

Extra time? They've got [g i n w s] and [e f a h t r e s]. They're....

1 💬 **Think and complete. Then talk with a friend.**

| tigers | snakes | penguins | monkeys | parrots | leopards | fish |

	They've got feathers.	They haven't got feathers.
ocean		
jungle		

2 **Make your lapbook. Find pictures or draw. Then write.**

My favourite animal habitat

1 What's your favourite habitat? _____

2 What animals live there? _____

3 What have they got? _____

4 What can they do? _____

Home-school link 📥 Tell your family about your favourite animal habitat.

47

6 Come on an adventure!

Let's review! PB p54–55

Think and write.
What animals have got fur?

_____ _____

_____ _____

Lesson 1 ➡ Vocabulary

1 Read and number.

1 skateboarding	2 rock-climbing	3 cycling	4 fishing
5 reading a map	6 building a den	7 sailing	8 drawing
9 having a picnic	10 doing a nature trail		

2 Look, read and write.

1 I'm <u>having a picnic.</u> I've got cheese and tomato sandwiches.

2 I'm _____ a picture of the park.

3 I'm _____. I'm lost!

4 I'm not _____,
I'm _____ to my
friend's house.

5 I'm not _____,
I'm _____
on the lake.

Tell me!
*What activities
are you good at?*

48

Extra time? What activities can you do at the beach?

1 Listen and circle.

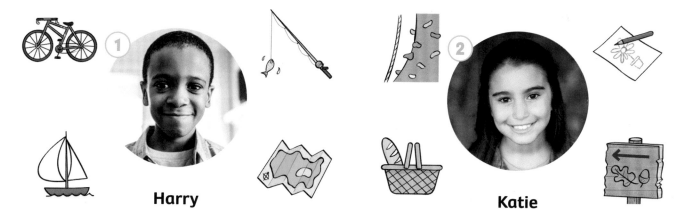

Harry   **Katie**

2 Look at Activity 1. Write.

> fishing   ~~cycling~~
> sailing   reading a map

> rock-climbing   having a picnic
> doing a nature trail   drawing

1 Harry <u>isn't cycling.</u>

He _____.

_____

He's _____.

2 Katie _____.

She _____.

_____

_____

I can **shine!**

3 💬 Look and write. Then tell a friend.

She isn't _____.

She's _____.

_____

_____

Extra time? Which new word is easy for you? Which is difficult for you?

1 **Look and write.**

| lake | mountain | river | island | ~~forest~~ | countryside |

1   _forest_

2 _____

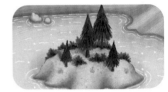

3 _____

4 _____

5 _____

6 _____

2   PB p66–67 ➡ **Read and number. Then write.**

| great | reading | doing | library | lake |

a   b   1   c   d

The _____ is behind these trees. Follow me!

He's _____ the map.

Wow! What a _____ adventure!

I can see the _____ and the countryside. What's that man _____?

I can shine!

Let's imagine!
*What do you think? The story is: OK ☆
good ☆☆   great ☆☆☆*

3 **Write for you.**

1 I think the adventure trail is _____.

   (fun) (scary) (exciting)

2 When it's raining, I like _____.

   (being outside) (staying at home) (having a picnic)

Extra time? How do the children help Thomas in the story?

1 **Look and write.**

1 What_'s_ she _doing?_
   She's _____ .

2 _____ he _____ ?
   _____

3 _Is_ he _cycling?_ No, _he isn't._
   _____ he _____ ?
   Yes, _____ .

4 _____ she _____ ?
   No, _____ .
   _____ she _____ ?
   Yes, _____ .

2 **Order and write. Then number.**

countryside. / the / go / Let's / to

_____ ☐

today? / like / weather / What's / the

_____ ☐

Let's build!
Choose a picture in Activity 1.
Ask and answer to guess which one.

's / sunny. / It

_____ ☐

I can shine! ✳

3 💬 **Think and write. Then ask and answer.**

What's _____ in the winter?

It's _____ .

 Let's _____ .

Pronunciation Circle the odd word out: snow show shower know

1 **Read and match.**

| ① | ② | ③ | ④ |

a

a It's windy. She's windsurfing on the lake.

b She's kayaking on the lake. It's a cool sport!

c He's in the mountains and he's skiing. He's having fun!

d She's sledging in the snow. It's scary, but it's exciting.

> *Do you prefer summer or winter activities? Why?*

2 🎧 **6.16** **Listen and write.**

① **Summer**

_____

_____

_____

_____

② **Winter**

_____

_____

_____

_____

3 **Write for you.**

<u>I like sledging in the mountains in the winter.</u>

I like _____ in the winter.

I like _____ in the summer.

Extra time? Can you go skiing when it isn't snowy?

1 **Read and tick (✓).**

BLOG

Home   About   Blog   ⋮

Home > Blog > Family trip

My family trip to the lake
by Tatiana

I am with my family. We're on a trip to a beautiful lake.
There's an island in the lake.
We're having lots of fun!
This is me! I'm sailing on the lake.
My brother is windsurfing.
My sister is cycling by the lake.

2 Give it a go **Plan your blog post.**

1 Where's your family trip? _____

2 Who's with you? _____

3 What activities are you doing? _____

4 What activities are your family doing? _____

I can shine!

3 **Write your blog post.**

BLOG   Home   About   Blog   ⋮

My family trip to _____ **, by** _____

_____

_____

_____

_____

_____

Check your work! Check your spelling. have ⟹ having cycle ⟹ cycling

1 **Find and circle. Then write.**

A	R	H	A	V	I	N	G	Q	C
M	E	R	H	B	C	W	Q	A	L
O	A	I	S	L	A	K	E	B	I
U	D	V	L	K	Q	P	D	N	M
N	I	E	D	O	I	N	G	M	B
T	N	R	Y	M	W	D	G	K	I
A	G	C	Y	C	L	I	N	G	N
I	D	R	A	W	I	N	G	P	G
N	W	X	Z	W	R	N	R	T	Y
S	C	B	U	I	L	D	I	N	G

1 He's <u>building</u> a den.

2 She's skiing in the _____.

3 He isn't _____ a nature trail.

4 She's _____ a picnic.

5 Is he _____ a map?

6 Is she sailing on the _____?

7 He isn't rock- _____.

8 She likes _____ pictures.

9 Is she _____ on her bike?

10 She's fishing next to the _____.

2 Write. Then listen and check.

1 He's in the <u>countryside.</u>

_____ skateboarding?

No, _____.

He's _____.

2 She's next to the _____.

_____ fishing?

No, _____.

_____

3 Write and answer for you. Then talk with a friend.

It's _____.

Let's go _____.

Extra time? You can do this with paper. You need a pencil.

1 💬 **Think and complete. Then talk with a friend.**

Choose two places near your home. What can you do there?

park town square beach countryside river mountains

Place	Summer activity	Winter activity

2 **Make your lapbook. Find pictures or draw. Then write.**

A place I like to visit

1 Choose a place from Activity 1. _____

2 What activities can you do there? _____

3 Who do you go with? _____

4 Can you go there in summer or winter? _____

5 What's the weather like? _____

Home-school link 📖 Tell your family about a place you like to visit.

55

1 Read and write.

BLOG

Home   About   **Blog**   ⋮

Kate Hall's nature trips

Kate is in the ¹[t a i m o n u n s] <u>mountains.</u>

She's ²[c o r k   g i n c i l b m]

_____ – _____.

She isn't ³[g w a n r i d] _____.

There are some ⁴[s p a d r e o l] _____.

They can't ⁵[f y l] _____ but they

⁶[n c a] _____ run.

They've got ⁷[s t o p s] _____.

They haven't got ⁸[p e r s t i s] _____.

2 🎧 6.22 **Look, read and circle. Listen and check. Then ask and answer.**

1 What's the **day / weather** like?

It's **snowy / windy**.

2 Shall we go **skiing / sailing**?

✗ **Yes, sure! / I'm not sure.**

3 OK. Let's go **fishing / windsurfing**.

✓ That's a **great / bad** idea!

3 Read and write.

1 __Have__ the parrots got fur?
  __No, they haven't.__

2 _____ they _____ feathers?
  _____

3 __Can__ they swim?
  _____

4 _____ fly?
  _____

5 __Is__ the boy having a picnic?
  _____

6 _____ he _____ a nature trail?
  _____

Mini-project

4 Imagine and write.

BLOG

	Blog ⋮

Kate is in _____ .

She's _____ .

She isn't _____ .

There are _____ .

They can _____ .

They've got _____ .

_____ .

Time to shine! ✴

5 Read and tick (✓). Tell your friend.

1 I can write a fact file about an animal. ☐

2 I can write a blog post about a school trip. ☐

3 I can talk about what animals have and haven't got. ☐

4 I can ask and answer about what friends are doing. ☐

My favourite song is in
Unit 5 ☐ Unit 6 ☐

My favourite story is in
Unit 5 ☐ Unit 6 ☐

6 Vote. Sing or act out.

 **from The Rise and Shine Library**

1 Think and write.

| History monkeys sailing sports centre Geography |
| storyteller reading corner snakes cinema fishing |

At school	In town	In the library	In the jungle	On the lake
_____	_____	_____	_____	_____
_____	_____	_____	_____	_____

2 Listen and number. Then write.

a  [1]

They've got ___fur.___
They can _____ high.

b  [ ]

Lena is _____ for animals.
Daniel isn't _____ a den.

c  [ ]

Rafa isn't very good at _____.
Does Lena like helping people?

_____

d  [ ]

There _____ a cinema.
Are there any police officers?

_____

3 Look at Activity 2. Ask and answer.

> Have the jerboas got fur?

> What's Daniel doing?

> Does Lena like doing crafts?

> Are there any shops in the town square?

4 Read and match.

1

2

3 [a]

4

a He likes drawing. He's good at painting. He doesn't like sports.

b She likes being outdoors. She loves animals. Her favourite school subject is Science.

c He's good at sports. He can run fast. His favourite subjects are PE and Maths.

d She likes taking photos and using computers. She's kind and clever.

5 Make your lapbook. Find pictures or draw. Then write.

My favourite things about The Rise and Shine Library

1 My favourite character in the Rise and Shine Library is _____.

2 I like _____ because _____.

3 My favourite new words are _____.

4 My favourite story is about _____.

5 I like the song from Unit _____.

6 My favourite fun fact is _____.

Home-school link Tell your family about The Rise and Shine Library.

59

World Teachers' Day

1 Look and write.

music room
ICT room
gym
classroom
~~canteen~~
science lab

1 _canteen_
2 _____
3 _____
4 _____
5 _____
6 _____

2 (8.04) Listen, order and write.

teachers / our / for

Hurray _____!

and / kind / help / they / us

They're _____.

World Kindness Day

3 Look and write.

care   give   ~~help~~
thank you   smile   talk

4 (8.08) Listen and circle.

It's World **Kindness /**

Helping Day!

Let's be **care / kind**,

Let's all **play / talk**.

1 _help_ someone

2 _____ someone a gift

3 _____ to a friend

4 say _____

5 _____

6 _____ about someone

World Book Day

5 Find and circle. Then write.

tellastory inventorkingqueencostumedressup

6 (8.12) Listen, order and write.

dress up / Book Day / for / World

Let's _____

_____!

hip-hip-hurray / choose /
a / costume –

Let's _____

_____!

1 _____ 2 _____

3 _____ 4 __tell a story__

5 _____ 6 _____

World Environment Day

7 Look and write.

turn off vegetables
plant walk
~~recycle~~ water

8 (8.16) Listen and match.

1 We can help   a to school.
2 We can grow   b off lights.
3 We can walk   c the planet!
4 We can turn   d vegetables.

1 __recycle__   2 grow _____

3 _____ 4 _____
to school   trees

5 _____ 6 _____
the plants   lights

Word connections

Word connections key

 Places

 People

 Activities

 Describing words

Welcome

Write your own new words!

Places in the library

courtyard
gallery
information desk
multimedia room
reading corner
study area

Library objects

beanbag
computer
poster
television

1 All about school!

School subjects

Art
Drama
English
Geography
History
ICT
Maths
Music
PE
Science

Routine actions

brush my teeth
go to bed
go to school
have breakfast
have a shower
wake up

2 Explore our town!

Places in town

bus stop
café
cinema
hospital
pharmacy

police station
shop
sports centre
supermarket
town square

What other places do you know?

Jobs

bus driver
doctor
librarian
police officer
shop assistant
waiter

3 Let's tell stories!

Book characters

astronaut
dragon
giant
monster
pirate

prince
princess
spy
storyteller
superhero

What other people do you know?

Adjectives

brave
clever
cute
kind
scary
strong

4 Party at the library!

Hobbies

acting
coding
having a party
juggling
learning an instrument
painting

playing chess
playing computer games
swapping cards
taking photos

Activities

being outside
doing crafts
doing sport
helping people
learning something new
using computers

5 Let's save our animals!

Animals

leopards	penguins
lions	rhinos
monkeys	snakes
pandas	tigers
parrots	zebras

Animal parts

feathers	stripes
fur	tail
spots	wings

What other describing words do you know?

6 Come on an adventure!

Outdoor activities

building a den
cycling
doing a nature trail
drawing
fishing
having a picnic
reading a map
rock-climbing
sailing
skateboarding

What other activities do you know?

Places in nature

countryside
forest
island
lake
mountain
river

What other places do you know?